UNMERCIFUL GOOD FORTUNE

Edwin Sánchez

BROADWAY PLAY PUBLISHING INC
224 E 62nd St, NY, NY 10065
www.broadwayplaypub.com
info@broadwayplaypub.com

Cover art from Northlight Theater production

First printing, this edition: January 2016

I S B N: 978-0-88145-645-5

Book design: Marie Donovan
Page make-up: Ventura & Indesign
Typeface: Palatino
Printed and bound in the U S A

ORIGINAL PRODUCTION

UNMERCIFUL GOOD FORTUNE premiered in Chicago in January of 1996 as a co-production of Northlight Theater (Russell Vandenbroucke, Artistic Director; Richard Friedman, Managing Director) and Victory Gardens Theater (Dennis Zacek, Artistic Director; John Walker, Managing Director), and as winner of the A T & T Onstage New Play Award. The cast and creative contributors were:

MARITZA CRUZ .... Sol Miranda
LUZ .... Carmen Roman
PITO .... Ernesto Gasco
PAUL LESLIE .... Jim Cantafio
JEREMY KIRKWOOD .... Clifton Williams
FATIMA GARCIA .... Denise Casano

Director .... Susana Tubert
Scenic design .... Mary Griswold
Costume design .... Claudia Boddy
Lighting design .... Todd Hensley
Sound design/original music .... Lindsay Jones
Production stage manager .... Amy A Field

CHARACTERS AND SETTING

MARITZA CRUZ, *26, single, assistant to the Bronx D A*
LUZ, *42,* MARITZA's *mother. She is bedridden.*
PITO, *77,* MARITZA's *father.*
PAUL LESLIE, *Bronx D A*
JEREMY KIRKWOOD, *Assistant Bronx D A*
FATIMA GARCIA, *28*

The scenes take place in the Bronx D A's office, the interrogation room, LUZ's *bedroom, and the living room.*

ACT ONE

(FATIMA, *a woman of about 28, wearing a fast food uniform, complete with hat, blankly faces the audience.*)

FATIMA: Will you be having fries with that?

(*Lights up on* MARITZA. *She is wearing a full slip and brushing her hair.* LUZ *is in her bed, staring straight ahead. Music begins to play softly in the background.* MARITZA *tries to feed* LUZ, *who refuses to open her mouth.*)

MARITZA: Come on, Mami. Just one. You ate for Leyda.

(*Enter* PITO, *looking for his granddaughter. He has a newspaper under his arm.*)

PITO: Marisol?

(MARITZA *hurries to the door, where she calls out.*)

MARITZA: Marisol. Grandpa's ready to take you to school now. Hurry up.

FATIMA: Will you be having fries with that?

(PITO *sits by* LUZ. *He takes her hand and kisses it. She does not react.* MARITZA *goes to her purse where she takes out some money.* PITO *begins to read the paper to* LUZ, *who takes the paper from him and hits him with it.* PITO *gently laughs.*)

MARITZA: Papi, here. Marisol needed money for school. I forget for what.

(PITO *takes the money.* MARITZA *is about to move the tray. She asks* LUZ.)

MARITZA: Do you want anymore?

PITO: She looks much better today.

(LUZ *begins to hum to herself.* MARITZA *gets her dress.*)

PITO: Ah, and Marisol is going to need money for lunch. She doesn't like the lunch you made for her.

(MARITZA, *with the dress half on, finishes putting it on as she goes for her purse. She gives* PITO *more money.* LUZ *laughs to herself.*)

MARITZA: She can buy lunch at school but please don't buy her anything when she gets out.

PITO: Sí, sí.

(PITO *kisses* LUZ *and* MARITZA *and exits.*)

FATIMA: Will you be having fries with that?

MARITZA: (*Calling through the door*) Marisol! (*To* LUZ) Did I give you this much trouble when I was growing up?

(LUZ *does not answer. With one hand she very gently touches her own face.*)

MARITZA: I'm late, Mami.

LUZ: Adiosito.

MARITZA: I'll try to be back early.

LUZ: Adiosito.

FATIMA: Will you be having fries with that?

(MARITZA *exits. At work, she stands in the doorway to her office.* PAUL LESLIE *is seated at her desk.*)

MARITZA: You wanted to see me, Sir?

(PAUL *studies her a moment.*)

MARITZA: Maritza Cruz. Assistant District Attorney. First year. This is my office.

PAUL: I wanted to see you yesterday.

MARITZA: I was in court all day.

PAUL: I'm sure you were very busy. Ms Cruz, what I have here is a complaint filed by one of your colleagues. This first-year punk felt you were interfering in the handling of his case. Unfortunately, he is the son of a friend of mine.

MARITZA: The suspect's mother was crying. I was (trying to help.)

PAUL: I don't like it when a rookie pulls some strings so that I have to get involved. I should never have to get involved, Cruz, and neither should you. There are twelve levels of management between us. Twelve. I only have to see you when I rubber stamp your hiring and when I'm reintroduced to you at the Christmas party. Now, I don't want to have to bury you in the library and I don't think you want that either. You're a very bright young woman, Cruz. Are you smirking at me?

MARITZA: No, Sir. *(Pause)* He was disrespectful, Sir.

PAUL: He was also dealing with a high-priority case. Do I have to define what that is for you?

MARITZA: I know what a high-priority case is, Sir.

PAUL: Good day, Cruz. *(He turns to leave.)*

MARITZA: The suspect was being tried, not his mother. And even though she's not one of your friends she still deserves to be treated with some respect. I'm sorry, Sir. I was out of line. I apologize.

(PAUL picks up his phone and dials an in-house number.)

PAUL: *(Into phone)* Jeremy, Maritza Cruz will be coming down to see you at the end of the day. Set her up in the library. No, it's okay. She volunteered. *(He hangs up. To* MARITZA:*)* Anything else?

MARITZA: No, Sir.

FATIMA: Will you be having fries with that?

(PAUL *exits.* MARITZA *goes to her desk. She puts her folders and her briefcase down. She picks up her briefcase and throws it on her desk.* JEREMY *enters with two coffees. She sees that he has witnessed her little outburst.*)

MARITZA: I'm sorry.

JEREMY: Please. In fact, take the one with the caffeine. You're a lot more fun when you got a little kick to you. So what'd you do? Word is you're persona non grata upstairs.

MARITZA: I was called on the carpet. No big deal.

JEREMY: It is a big deal. I was here for three years before he knew my name. And that's just the way I liked it. Don't make enemies, Maritza.

MARITZA: I would never be disrespectful to him, he's my superior. I wasn't raised that way.

JEREMY: Okay, so you just do your penance, a couple of days in library hell, and he'll hopefully forget all about it and then we can plot some way to put you back in his good graces.

MARITZA: I don't care if I'm in his good graces.

FATIMA: Will you be having fries with that?

JEREMY: Maritza, I'm just trying to be your friend here. I know your mother has been, is very sick but learn where to take your aggression out. Don't commit career suicide. Never insult the big guy. He always wins. He will always win. You want to take it out on somebody, take it out on me.

MARITZA: Thank you. (*Silence*)

JEREMY: How is she?

MARITZA: The same. She lies in her bed mixing memories and fantasies all day long until I don't know what's what. She'll tell me things she expects me to remember and she's so sure of them that I begin to think that maybe I've forgotten pieces of my life.

JEREMY: Which pieces?

MARITZA: The fun pieces that only she can remember.

FATIMA: Will you be having fries with that?

(LUZ's *bedroom.* LUZ *is, as always, in bed. She is a very attractive woman of 42.)*

LUZ: Why don't you ever come to see me?

MARITZA: I was here this morning, Mami. I fed you breakfast.

LUZ: Leyda fed me breakfast.

MARITZA: Let's change your clothes, Mami. Get you into something nice for dinner.

FATIMA: Will you be having fries with that?

MARITZA: Comb out your hair. *(Laughs)* I remember when you used my lint brush on your hair. Remember, Mami?

LUZ: Of course I remember.

MARITZA: What do you want to wear tonight?

LUZ: I want Leyda to dress me.

MARITZA: Leyda's not here, Mami.

LUZ: She's the fun one. I want her to dress me. And to brush my hair. I love you, Maritza, but you depress me.

MARITZA: Mami, I'm not in the mood for Leyda tonight.

LUZ: You go get her, I'll wait.

(MARITZA *puts her head in her hands.)*

MARITZA: I'm so tired.

LUZ: You too? Even with all this bed rest—

LUZ & MARITZA: I'm so tired.

(MARITZA *raises her head. She has "become" Leyda for* LUZ.)

MARITZA: Okay, girlfriend, we've got to get you ready for tonight. The sailors are in port and honey, they are screaming out your name.

LUZ: *(Laughs)* Oh, they are not.

MARITZA: Come on, you old whore. Let's get you into something with cleavage. Something that whispers "shore leave".

LUZ: You go by yourself.

MARITZA: I can't handle all those men by myself, Luz. You gotta help me.

LUZ: You think they still want me?

MARITZA: They all want you. (*She very gently begins to undress* LUZ.) No matter where you go you're always the center of attention.

(LUZ *laughs. She grimaces in pain when* MARITZA *raises one of her arms.*)

MARITZA: Sorry.

LUZ: Maybe we'll meet an admiral. He'll invite us back on the ship and give a party for us. I'd love to be able to say I danced on water. Do you have a lot of boyfriends?

MARITZA: Do you want to take a rest now?

LUZ: No, it's okay. Do men like you?

MARITZA: Like mother, like daughter. You are looking at 100% man candy. Men throw themselves at my feet. Well, the ones with bad aim do. The bright ones go for the bull's eye. Men would kill for us, Mami. It's our curse. So young, so beautiful.

LUZ: Maritza doesn't like men, you know? She can have any man she wants. I mean, she's pretty. Not like you and me, of course, but intelligent pretty.

MARITZA: Yeah, she's a bright one.

LUZ: Talk to her. Whenever I bring it up with her she gets so angry, you know? *(Laughs)* She's ruining our track record.

MARITZA: I'll be right back.

FATIMA: Will you be having fries with that?

LUZ: Aren't you going to brush my hair? Give me a couple of spit curls.

MARITZA: Yeah, yeah. I gotta see about dinner. You practice leaning against lamp posts or something.

(MARITZA exits to living room. Her father, PITO, is sitting on the sofa. He is 77 to LUZ's 42. He is dressed formally and sits with his hat in his lap.)

MARITZA: La bendición.

PITO: Dios me la bendiga.

MARITZA: Where's Marisol?

PITO: She's in her room. I bought her some pizza.

FATIMA: Will you be having fries with that?

MARITZA: I was going to make dinner for her.

PITO: Now you don't have to. How's your mother?

MARITZA: I'm taking a Mami break.

PITO: Can I feed her?

MARITZA: She's on the Leyda jag. She only wants Leyda tonight.

PITO: You're a good daughter. You can't see it now,
I know, but Luz was the prettiest girl in Isabela. So shy.
She would walk through the town square with her
sisters. All of them dressed in white. Like angels.

MARITZA: Have you eaten yet?

PITO: I was considered by everyone to be a very serious,
very honorable man—No, but I'm not really hungry—
I was forty-seven years old. Divorced. Used to living
alone, and this—

MARITZA: I'm making stew for Mami. You want some?

PITO: Are you going to let me finish my story? Young
girl enters my life. This angel sent to me from God
himself to end my loneliness. And now God wants her
back. *(He begins to cry.)* Why does God put us on earth
to suffer?

MARITZA: Papi, come on. Look, I'm going to start
dinner. Why don't you come into the kitchen with
me and tell me stories about when you were growing
up in Puerto Rico. Come on.

PITO: Are you finished with your mother?

MARITZA: She can wait a little bit, just for tonight.
You can help me cook.

PITO: Men don't cook.

MARITZA: Okay, you can watch. And talk to me, Papi.

LUZ: *(V/O)* Leyda—

FATIMA: Will you be having fries with that?

LUZ: *(V/O)* Leyda, come brush my hair.

(The office area. MARITZA *is already at work.* JEREMY *enters.)*

JEREMY: Thank me later. Grab your things, we're outta
her.

MARITZA: Wait a second, what do you mean?

JEREMY: We're going to an arraignment. I need somebody who speaks Spanish and I can't find a translator.

MARITZA: Santiago is in his cubicle.

JEREMY: Goodness me, I must have missed him. So again, all the translators were out, so I had to take you.

MARITZA: I'm not going to lie.

JEREMY: That's okay, I'll lie for both of us. They just brought in a girl who worked in a fast food restaurant and poisoned the burgers.

MARITZA: She did what?

JEREMY: She worked at "Country Joe's Burgers" off Fordham Road. She had been there for a little less than a week. Got there extra early, most days. Kept to herself. We don't know how she did it, but she managed to lace a batch of hamburgers with poison. We are waiting for more info on the poison. Twelve people reported dead since yesterday. The papers are going to eat her up. I think I saw Paul actually crack a smile. This could be a major case for the man so he's probably in a real forgiving mood right now.

MARITZA: And?

JEREMY: And? You're welcome.

(The interrogation room. FATIMA *is seated, wearing handcuffs.* PAUL, MARITZA, *and* JEREMY *sit at a table, a few feet away from her.)*

PAUL: What is she? Twelve?

JEREMY: Twenty?

MARITZA: Twenty-eight.

*(*FATIMA *smiles at this last number.)*

JEREMY: An old woman neighbor of hers kept crossing herself and telling us she's a witch.

MARITZA: *(Dismissively)* Oh, God.

PAUL: *(To* MARITZA*)* You live in the Bronx, Ms Cruz, have you ever seen her around?

MARITZA: *(She rolls her eyes.)* No, Sir.

PAUL: She offered no resistance on her arrest. Just raised her hands and said—

FATIMA: *(Under* PAUL *line)* Ya era hora.

PAUL: "It's about time" in Spanish.

JEREMY: How did the police even find out?

PAUL: The mother of a little girl who died called in.

MARITZA: A little girl?

PAUL: Eight years old. *(Pause)* Ask her if she wants to speak to you in Spanish.

MARITZA: *(To* FATIMA*)* ¿Quieres hablar conmigo en Español? *(No reply from* FATIMA.*)* Soy Maritza Cruz.

FATIMA: *(Offering her hand)* Gimme your hand. *(*MARITZA *does not.)* Gimme your hand.

*(*MARITZA *still does not.* PAUL *intercedes and offers his hand.)*

PAUL: Paul Leslie. District Attorney for the Bronx.

*(*PAUL *and* FATIMA *shake hands.* PAUL *motions to* JEREMY, *who rises and joins them.)*

JEREMY: Jeremy Kirkwood, deputy district attorney.

*(*JEREMY *and* FATIMA *shake hands.* FATIMA *again offers her hand to* MARITZA. *There is an awkward pause.* MARITZA *slowly offers her hand.* MARITZA *and* FATIMA *barely touch hands.)*

FATIMA: Why you? You're not like me. You are nothing like me!

(JEREMY *enters* MARITZA's *work area.*)

JEREMY: Why is it, no matter what time I get here, you always beat me?

MARITZA: It's the only time I can do my prep work. It's quiet.

JEREMY: Tell me about it. I got three kids.

MARITZA: My daughter's six years old and she can already zone me out. Last night I'm tucking her in and she faced the wall.

JEREMY: I would have flipped the mattress over with the little rug rat on it. Bet you cried.

MARITZA: Yeah, well. She wants to go live with her father.

(*The interrogation room.* FATIMA *is seated at a table with two chairs facing each other.* JEREMY *enters.*)

JEREMY: What's your Legal Aid counselor doing outside?

FATIMA: Oh, is he outside?

JEREMY: He won't come in.

FATIMA: We made a deal.

JEREMY: I can't talk to you unless he's here.

FATIMA: It's okay. I trust you.

JEREMY: Yeah, well, my boss wouldn't feel too comfortable about this.

FATIMA: He's an asshole.

JEREMY: Uh, I have to tape everything you say.

(JEREMY *places a small tape recorder on the table.* FATIMA *picks it up and speaks directly into it.*)

FATIMA: Your boss is an asshole. Too bad this thing can't record you nodding.

JEREMY: *(Reprimanding her)* Fatima.

FATIMA: *(Imitating him)* Jeremy. *(Pause)* So, is it always noisy like this?

JEREMY: You get used to it. It becomes a hum.

FATIMA: Oh, I like it. It's the quiet that sucks. I need noise around me. Noise at least means people are around. Too quiet, you think too much. Hey, can you get me a T V?

JEREMY: There's one in the community room.

FATIMA: Yeah, well, they're always watching soaps. They get into fights about whether it should be in English or Spanish.

JEREMY: I'm sorry. There's nothing I can do.

FATIMA: Cool. *(Pause)* So who gets these tapes? Your boss?

JEREMY: Everything we say, he knows.

(FATIMA *smiles.*)

FATIMA: Cool.

JEREMY: Do you want to talk to me?

FATIMA: I want to talk to Maritza.

JEREMY: I thought you didn't like her.

FATIMA: Maritza or nobody.

JEREMY: Let's get this straight from this point forward, okay? I like being a nice guy, and I'd rather we did this nice but if we have to do it the other way, that's fine too. You're in no position to be laying down rules. The rules are made by me, period. You got a problem with that? I'll just talk to your Legal Aid rep.

FATIMA: No you won't. You know why? 'Cause I'm the one who's gonna get you a promotion and Mr Asshole a lot of free press. Something he really likes, you know. It's all in your hands. But the only person I'll talk to is Maritza. You wanna see a trick, sure you do. Gimme your hand.

(JEREMY awkwardly does. FATIMA turns off the recorder.)

JEREMY: Look, it doesn't really make me look too great with my boss if I have you calling the shots. Whatever you want to tell her you can tell me.

(He reaches for the recorder in order to turn it on. FATIMA pulls it out of his reach.)

FATIMA: If you don't break up with this woman you're seeing she's going to get pregnant. Your wife already suspects something, but she's playing it real cool. This other woman is going to wreck your life if you let her.

(JEREMY jerks his hand away and stares at her.)

FATIMA: I didn't think the recorder should be on for that. That's nobody's business but yours. Her name is Wanda.

(JEREMY slowly stands. FATIMA hands him the recorder.)

FATIMA: See what you can do about getting me Maritza. Oh, and like this, with no guards. Girl talk don't need no chaperone.

(JEREMY stumbles out. FATIMA makes a gun out of her hand, fires it after him, and blows on it. Lights dim. In the background MARITZA is picking up Marisol's toys.)

MARITZA: Marisol. Marisol, come pick up your toys. I'm not going to clean up your messes anymore. You make them, you clean them up. Marisol!

(The interrogation room. PAUL enters carrying a portable T V.)

PAUL: A little...loan for you. Thought you might like to have your own T V for awhile. You know, there are a lot of privileges you can earn with the right cooperation. You are a very bright young woman, Fatima. Did I say your name right? (FATIMA *does not answer.*) You really gave old Jeremy a fright, didn't you? He's a real stickler for rules. I'm a little more flexible. Especially for the right person. For instance, you. You talk directly to me and I become Mr Cooperation. Have we got a deal? (FATIMA *does not answer.*) I take that to mean that you don't care to see Ms Cruz, either.

(FATIMA *finally looks at him.*)

PAUL: Deal directly with me, talk directly with me, and I'll allow you to see Ms Cruz. What do you say? Shall we shake on it?

(*They do.* FATIMA *pushes the T V, screen first, to the floor, where it shatters.*)

PAUL: Are you out of your fucking mind?!

FATIMA: Maritza. Oh, and by the way, you'll be completely bald by the time you're fifty-seven.

(PAUL *catches himself as his hand involuntarily goes up to his head.*)

FATIMA: Part it on the other side. It'll disguise it better.

PAUL: Kiss daylight goodbye, Ms Garcia.

FATIMA: So tell me, why you still in the Bronx, Paul?

PAUL: There's a car outside waiting to take you to Riker's.

FATIMA: It's not fair that someone as good as you should be wasting themselves here. It's almost a sin. I'm gonna get you out of the Bronx. Me. I'm gonna make it so that six days from now the higher ups are gonna have to eat your shit for breakfast, lunch, and dinner.

PAUL: I think you're confusing yourself with someone who matters.

FATIMA: You called Morris, your boss, two days ago and today was when he finally got around to returning your phone call. You don't think that's disrespectful? He's afraid of you and he's gonna do everything he can to keep you down. But he don't have me, you do, and you only get me once in a lifetime, Paul. So what you gonna do, use me or waste me?

PAUL: What do you want?

FATIMA: To meet with Maritza. Alone.

(PAUL *reaches the door.*)

PAUL: Have a good life, Ms Garcia.

FATIMA: "Crusading Bronx D A Fights Evil". That'll be your first headline. Six days of them, Paul. The next one will have your name in it. Like it?

(PAUL *looks at her, picks up the box of the broken T V, and exits.*)

FATIMA: Yeah, well, I thought you would.

(The interrogation room)

JEREMY: What I got was exactly what you heard on the tape. What I'm saying is that this is going to be a major case and I think we should have as much information going into the court room as possible, and if talking to Maritza loosens this nut case's tongue, well then fine. Let's go with it.

PAUL: Why do you think she wants to see you?

MARITZA: I don't know, Sir.

PAUL: Okay, Ms Cruz, have a first meeting with her tomorrow. Maritza, this comes under the heading of "high priority". *(He exits.)*

MARITZA: Are you okay about this?

JEREMY: Yeah, sure. She took my hand and she knew me. I mean she knew me. It was like I was feeding her information about me. She knew everything.

(LUZ's bedroom. MARITZA is giving her a sponge bath.)

LUZ: Nothing she ever did bothered me as much as when she got herself pregnant.

MARITZA: Who?

LUZ: Maritza, who else? Falls for the first man to look at her sweetly. For pete's sakes, where's the girl's brain?

MARITZA: Maybe she was in love, Luz.

LUZ: Que love ni love. We can fall in love every night, can't we, Leyda?

MARITZA: You said it, Luz.

LUZ: If you're gonna get swept off your feet every time a man sweet talks to you, forget about it. I wanted her to live, have boyfriends. Not wake up one day with a screaming kid on her hip and no taste of life. Ay, Leyda. You and me are the smart ones. Never let a man own you. And the second he says he loves you, drop him.

MARITZA: Amen to that, Luz.

LUZ: You know, I wish I could talk to your sister like this, but she won't let me. Her face gets tight, then it closes up and she's judging. She, who hasn't lived, is judging me. Leyda, you and me are gonna go away.

MARITZA: Oh yeah, where to?

LUZ: Anywhere but here. And you know, I'll never come back to the Bronx again. Not even to visit. But we won't take Maritza with us. She just don't know how to have a good time. I would do everything differently. Ven acá, you know what really makes me angry about Maritza?

MARITZA: No, what?

LUZ: She settled. First man, first job. No sense of adventure. She's just like her father.

PITO: I killed myself to make a safe place for my little family. Worked and worked and worked.

LUZ: I want to be an evil woman. You'll be my partner in crime, huh, Leyda?

MARITZA: New York watch out.

LUZ: Que New York. The world better watch out.

(MARITZA *exits.*)

LUZ: All those other ladies will have to eat my dust as my five-inch sling backs tear up the dance floor. Rumba, Mambo, Cha Cha Cha. The back of my neck is sopping wet, I push my hair up, and every man is staring at me as it cascades down my naked and glistening neck. I dare them not to want me.

PITO: My little virgin in white.

(*The interrogation room.* FATIMA *is seated.* PAUL *and* MARITZA *enter.*)

PAUL: Ms Garcia, Ms Cruz.

FATIMA: Ms Cruz. Let's get to know each other. (*To* PAUL) You're dismissed.

(PAUL *stands there.*)

FATIMA: Beat it. Oh, "Bronx D A Vows Revenge". Now get out. Yeah, I know, you want your name in it. Billing. It's all about billing.

PAUL: Don't push your luck.

FATIMA: The first headline was right, wasn't it?

PAUL: This is not about the headlines.

FATIMA: Please don't insult my intelligence. I used to spit on guys like you in the subway and my aim is as good as it ever was. I may not know my syntax and my use of double negatives may get on your nerves, but please don't insult my intelligence. And that smile of condescension can be slapped clear off your face.

PAUL: We are not on the subway now. All you are here and now is a loud-mouthed girl.

FATIMA: Don't you mean spic?

PAUL: No, I don't mean spic. I don't use that word.

FATIMA: Ooh no, you mama raised herself a liberal.

MARITZA: I'll have a full report on your desk in the morning, Sir.

(PAUL *leaves.*)

FATIMA: Aren't we the good little girl?

(MARITZA *puts a tape recorder on the desk and turns it on.*)

MARITZA: Do you prefer Fatima or Ms Garcia?

(FATIMA *turns off the recorder.*)

FATIMA: Gimme your hand.

(MARITZA *turns on the recorder. She takes a list of questions and places it in front of herself.*)

MARITZA: I have a list of questions I'd like to ask you.

(FATIMA *again turns off the recorder.*)

FATIMA: Gimme your hand.

(MARITZA *turns on the recorder and places it close to herself on the desk.*)

MARITZA: Can I please have your full name, starting with the last name first.

FATIMA: ...Garcia, Fatima. Please turn off the recorder. It's the only favor I'll ask you.

MARITZA: My boss (expects me to follow procedure.)

FATIMA: —will be happy with a headline per day.

(MARITZA *turns off the recorder and places it on the table.*)

FATIMA: You can throw away your questions. I got nothing to hide from you. We go way back. Gimme your hand.

(MARITZA *does not.*)

MARITZA: It'll go a lot faster if we can keep to some sort of rules.

FATIMA: You know how a splinter feels? You know the relief you feel when you finally get the tweezers just so and you pull the splinter out? The wound is still there but the hurt has been pulled out. I have this splinter in my heart. Come on, just let me hold your hand. Just once. I can't trust you if you won't trust me. If I can't see into your life what's the big deal? I'm just gonna hold your hand. Pretend it's your boyfriend.

MARITZA: When did I lose control with you?

FATIMA: The second you came in. *(She turns on the recorder.)* So, Ms Cruz, as a gesture of good will you were saying you were going to let me hold your hand.

(MARITZA *gives her an angry look.* FATIMA *turns off the recorder.*)

FATIMA: I didn't want this thing. And I sure as hell never called it a gift. My mother said my father was scared of me when I was a little girl. I would stare at people. Like I'm three months old and I'm staring into people's faces. Everybody in my mother's family did la brujería. But when I got to be thirteen I realized that they were like grooming me to be the child bride of Satan. Later for that shit. I ran away.

MARITZA: What did you do?

FATIMA: Lived on the streets for three years. That's when I joined my girl gangs. A girl's gotta have herself some representation on the street; you know it's the truth. I would never have chosen you. Anybody but you. You're too close to call. And now only you can pull this splinter from my heart. Only you can give me relief.

(MARITZA *gets up and collects her things.*)

MARITZA: If you have anything to tell me I'll be back tomorrow. Otherwise, you're just wasting my time. And yours.

FATIMA: I can't do this alone, Maritza.

(MARITZA *exits. She has forgotten the recorder.*
FATIMA *turns it on and speaks softly into the microphone.*)

FATIMA: Boo.

(The living room)

PITO: I regret the day I left the island. I should have stayed. You come looking for a better way of life not knowing you're leaving the best behind.

MARITZA: Why didn't you go back, Papi?

PITO: Pride. I didn't want your mother's family to think I was a failure. New York was supposed to be paved in gold. A perfect place for my girl.

MARITZA: She was just a girl.

PITO: She still played with dolls.

MARITZA: How did you know she was the one?

PITO: I don't know.

MARITZA: I mean, you had other girlfriends before, right? Why didn't you marry any of the others?

(PITO *takes* MARITZA'*s arm. He leads her in a slow circular walk around the room.*)

PITO: In Isabela, girls could only go out on Sunday. Rest of the week they went to school, helped their mothers. But Sundays, in the afternoon, their fathers would take them to the town square. The old men would sit and the girls would walk around the square. Supposedly talking with each other, but flirting like crazy.

MARITZA: With who?

PITO: With the boys who were still in their church clothes. Two groups walking around the square, with the girls' fathers watching. This was back when old men were respected. They would watch and if their daughter looked at the wrong boy it was suddenly time to go home. Some of the older girls wore a little make-up, some of the older boys were a little brash, but it was a very sweet time back then. Your mother was with her three sisters, she was the baby of the family. Twelve. Her sisters played with their eyes, played with their hair. Coquetry in a woman is a beautiful thing. Luz wore no make-up and her dress seemed to be a hand-me-down from her older sister. But once I saw her, there was no other woman in the square.

MARITZA: She was a girl.

PITO: And I was a forty-seven-year-old man. I didn't talk to her for a full year. I would just follow her with my eyes. I never thought she would notice me. At thirteen she said to me, "Good day." I thought my heart would burst. It was then I would permit myself to walk alongside her in the square. That was the happiest time in my life. Me pesa el corazon.

MARITZA: Sssh, Papi.

PITO: When she dies I'm going to kill myself.

MARITZA: Don't say that.

PITO: God can't punish me anymore. He's taking away the thing I love most in the world. You know, when

she's sleeping and the pain has left her face, I see
the girl I fell in love with. Maritza, when she goes,
wherever she goes, I must go with her. I promised her
parents I would protect her from all harm. I'm going
with her.

(The next day. The interrogation room. FATIMA *at table.
Enter* MARITZA.*)*

FATIMA: Maritza.

MARITZA: Ms Garcia. Are you ready for me today?

FATIMA: I was ready for you yesterday. *(She has placed
the recorder by the door. She points to it.)* You forgot your
recorder. It's over there by the door. I saved it for you.

*(*MARITZA *retrieves the recorder.)*

FATIMA: Nice legs. Nice walk. You don't like me,
do you? ¿Te caigo mal, verdad?

MARITZA: You have no previous record. Am I correct in
assuming that?

FATIMA: Mmm hmm. What do your friends call you?

MARITZA: Mary.

FATIMA: Too white. I bet you've passed yourself
off as white a couple of times. How about it? Best
performance by a spic in a white role, the winner is....
You can even hold on to your temper like a white
person.

MARITZA: Do you want to see me get angry? I was
under the impression you wanted to talk about what
you had done. How you killed twelve innocent people.

FATIMA: Twenty-eight.

MARITZA: What?

FATIMA: "Fatima Offs Twenty-eight Who Wanted to Die". That'll be tomorrow's headline. Now all you have to do is earn it. Gimme your hand.

MARITZA: How did you find twenty-eight people who wanted to die?

FATIMA: Are you kidding, this is New York. Hand, sweet Mary. You gotta earn that headline.

MARITZA: Again, how did you know they wanted to die?

FATIMA: When I hold somebody's hand I can read their life. I can see everything. It just is. Now gimme your fucking hand.

(MARITZA *does not.*)

MARITZA: Are you currently taking any drugs?

FATIMA: Get the fuck out. When you're willing to do a little hand holding with the accused then you can come back. Oh, and Miss Legal Diva, explain to your boss how you lost his headlines for him. (MARITZA *does not leave.*) You're not gonna go away, are you, Maritza? Please, Maritza.

(*The living room.* MARITZA *enters, trying not to be noticed.* PITO *is half asleep.*)

PITO: Maritza? Maritza? (*He wanders out.*)

(MARITZA *looks after her father as he leaves.*)

MARITZA: Not tonight, Papi. I can't. I have nothing left. (*She is about to walk to her room when she hears her mother weeping in pain through the door. Her briefcase falls from her hands and she covers her ears with her hands.*) Dear God, please take her away. If all she's going to do is suffer, take her away. You have no right to make her suffer. Please. End it.

(*The interrogation room.* MARITZA *and* FATIMA.)

FATIMA: My story, by Fatima Garcia as told to Maritza
Cruz. I belonged to the Cherries. We were the female
counterpart to the Chicos until one day we had a big
fight and we beat the hell out of them. There was no
way we were gonna take any shit from them after that.
Did you ever get into any fights or were you always the
good little girl?

MARITZA: I wasn't a threat to society, no.

FATIMA: I used to keep a razor blade in my mouth.
Between my upper gum and the inside of my mouth.
Taught myself. Good for fights.

MARITZA: Weren't you afraid you would cut yourself?

FATIMA: Cut yourself once you don't do it again. I could
have full conversations with it in my mouth. No one
knew. Maybe I have it in my mouth right now.
That scare you, Maritza?

MARITZA: No.

FATIMA: So it's okay if I put my hand in my mouth,
huh? I mean, you ain't gonna call the guard or shit like
that. Do you think your boss would let me do this?
(She reaches her hand into her mouth and pulls out a razor
blade. She takes it and puts it in the palm of her hand.)
One two three. (She squeezes it in the palm of her hand.)

(MARITZA gets up.)

FATIMA: Sit down if you don't want me to use this on
you.

MARITZA: You're hurting yourself.

FATIMA: Squeeze it nice and tight and the blood don't
flow. Now comes the dare. I used to do this with my ex,
Coco. You squeeze and squeeze until one of you can't
take it anymore. Or passes out.

MARITZA: Let go of it. Open your hand.

FATIMA: Gimme your hand.

MARITZA: Put the razor on the table right now.

FATIMA: *(Sings)* I want to hold your hand, hand, hand, hand. I want to hold your hand.

MARITZA: Knock it off! Guard!

FATIMA: If he comes in I'll kill myself. Quick, who was the cutest Beatle?

MARITZA: What? Uh, Paul.

FATIMA: Wrongo. John. Say John.

MARITZA: John.

(The guard is about to enter.)

FATIMA: Don't let him in or I'll slit my wrists.

MARITZA: Wait outside, please.

FATIMA: Gimme your hand. It only hurts if you let it hurt. Gimme your hand. I won't cut you. I swear to God I won't cut you.

(MARITZA thrusts out her hand. FATIMA clasps it tightly in hers.)

FATIMA: You're the one who's gonna pull the splinter from my heart.

(MARITZA's look of dread turns to one of disbelief as she pulls her hand away.)

FATIMA: It's gum foil wrapper, girlfriend, where the fuck was I gonna get a razor here?

MARITZA: I don't care what information you think you're dealing with. As far as I'm concerned you can rot in here.

FATIMA: I got to hold your hand, Maritza. I know you now.

(MARITZA turns to leave.)

FATIMA: What do you think I know? What's the worse thing I could know?

MARITZA: Nothing.

FATIMA: Everything. Who's Leyda?

MARITZA: ...I thought you knew everything.

FATIMA: Okay, she's your twin sister who died at birth. Sometimes you gotta act like her for your mother. Why? *(Silence)* Hey, if I'm wrong just tell me. You know, you're pretty good at blocking me. The best. Ain't nobody a mystery to me once I take their hand, but you, you doing like body blocks on my psyche. How'd you get to be so good?

MARITZA: So every time a customer would come in you would shake their hand and try to, what? Envision their lives?

FATIMA: Ooh, segue baby, segue.

MARITZA: And depending on what you saw you would give them a—

FATIMA: Fatima Poisoned Special.

MARITZA: Did you ever think you might be wrong?

FATIMA: Was I wrong just now?

MARITZA: Who gave you the right to play God?

FATIMA: Oh no, I don't play God. God is like into this Russian roulette shit. You could be standing there, not doing nothing, and God would zap you out. I was doing public service.

MARITZA: Without giving them the benefit of a choice?

FATIMA: Ask me what I saved them from. How come you don't ask me that? I know them all by name. Pick a name from your file. Ask me about Viginia Lopez. Eight years old and her father's sex toy for the last two years. You don't know what the fuck it was like to take her hand and see that life. Eugene Patz was going to jump into the subway tracks, he just found out he had AIDS. Sonia Rambal was homeless, she was not gonna last another winter. I'm talking about people who wanted to die. No one took care of them.

MARITZA: So you decided you would.

FATIMA: One less sad person. I take their hand and I can feel the tears on the inside of their eyes. Why do they gotta suffer so much? Little girls with old women faces. What if you had no future? If this was as good as it got? Ever.

MARITZA: You still had no right.

FATIMA: Well, it's too late. I can kill 'em but I can't bring 'em back.

MARITZA: What if you were wrong?

FATIMA: I never was.

MARITZA: How the hell do you know? You're wearing your polyester uniform with a funny hat and deciding who lives or dies. There's no remorse, no guilt.

FATIMA: They would thank me if they could.

MARITZA: Well, guess what, they can't. Even if they were suffering they might have wanted to live.

FATIMA: No they didn't.

MARITZA: You can't know that for sure.

FATIMA: My personal hell is that I do.

MARITZA: All knowing, huh? What's your level of education?

FATIMA: I don't see what the hell—

MARITZA: It's a very simple question.

FATIMA: Yeah, I know it's a simple question.

MARITZA: I would just like to know what your qualifications are for deciding who lives and dies. I mean, is it an elementary school drop-out who's making these decisions? Did you take a correspondence course? Who?!

FATIMA: I guess the same person who told you you were better than me.

MARITZA: I used to get beat up by girls like you. The tough girls. The gang around my block was called "Las Hembras". I could count on their making fun of me every single day. If one of them dropped a pen they would just say, "pick it up", and I would. With a smile on my lips. The smile of submission. "Why do you think you're better than us?" Smack-smack-smack. "Who told you to talk?" Smack-smack-smack. I took it all. I never snapped. I think about those girls now, "Las Hembras". Where are they now? Dead. Welfare mothers. No future. I saw one of them on the subway and I held her stare. I would not look down until she did. Smack-smack-smack. She did. Does this mean I won?

FATIMA: And if she didn't look down, were you ready to go for it on the I R T?

MARITZA: She didn't have the guts to find out.

FATIMA: Tough talk.

MARITZA: Life beat the guts out of her.

FATIMA: Exactly, life. Not you.

(MARITZA *shoots her an angry look.*)

FATIMA: Not to say that you couldn't.

MARITZA: I would have preferred running into an old friend. And she and I would have a lot of catching up to do. We had been good friends. Life had been sweet. We had shared secrets and good times. Old school friends.

FATIMA: She wore cheap brightly colored clothing.

MARITZA: She would ask me to be the godmother of her child.

FATIMA: She got knocked up again.

MARITZA: A girl she would name after me.

FATIMA: While she's got two brats with dry snot that she can't control running all over the subway car.

MARITZA: So good to see you again. Smack-smack-smack.

FATIMA: I'm sorry. You were right. I should have been like you, Maritza.

MARITZA: Call me. Here's my business card.

FATIMA: I'm sorry.

MARITZA: Soon.

FATIMA: I'm sorry.

MARITZA: Fuck you.

FATIMA: Your hand in marriage, Ms Cruz.

(*This last statement jolts* MARITZA. *She stands and leaves.*)

FATIMA: Hey!

(*The living room.* MARITZA *is there.* PITO *enters.*)

PITO: Marisol just leave?

MARITZA: It's better this way. She'll get to miss me. She'll appreciate me more.

PITO: How can a daughter not appreciate—

MARITZA: Papi, please.

PITO: —her own mother. You should have married her father.

MARITZA: I'm going out for a while.

PITO: Marriage is a beautiful thing, Maritza. I felt so honored to be given your mother. I was the first man in her life, and if her death gives me any consolation it's that it guarantees I'll be the only man in her life.

MARITZA: And if she wanted more? Was Mami the only woman in your life?

PITO: Of course not.

MARITZA: How would you feel if she had been?

PITO: I would be honored. Before I met your mother I spent my entire life searching for her.

MARITZA: Me too.

(The interrogation room. FATIMA *is seated. Enter* JEREMY.*)*

FATIMA: I kind of figured you would be back. You want to know more, don't you? Yeah, it's kind of addictive.

JEREMY: Have you been reading the guards' fortunes?

*(*FATIMA *stares at him.)*

JEREMY: Do they believe you?

FATIMA: Do you? Let's cut to the chase. Gimme your hand. (JEREMY *doesn't move.)* Hey, I'm a very busy woman. Gimme a hand here. I can't do it all by myself.

*(*JEREMY *gives her his hand.)*

JEREMY: You know, you were so wrong in what you told me last time I thought I'd give you another chance.

FATIMA: Mmm hmm, spare me.

(They hold hands.)

JEREMY: How does it work?

FATIMA: It's like seeing a movie of your life. Only I can flash forward or go back.

JEREMY: Tell me something from my past.

(FATIMA *gives him a condescending look.*)

JEREMY: You know, just so I can see you're on the level.

FATIMA: I don't do "Bewitched".

JEREMY: ...Don't hurt me.

FATIMA: Hurting you is what I do best. Truth hurts. Life's a bitch.

(MARITZA *enters.*)

FATIMA: Oops, sorry, Jeremy. We're gonna have to put your future on hold.

JEREMY: I was, uh.... (*He exits.*)

FATIMA: Odiame por piedad yo te lo pido. Odiame sin medida ni clemencia.

MARITZA: What's that?

FATIMA: Oh, come on. You're not going to tell me your mother didn't play this song to death.

(MARITZA *smiles in recognition.*)

FATIMA: Hoy yo quiero más que indiferencia. Jump in.

FATIMA & MARITZA: Porque el rencor hierre menos que el olvido.

FATIMA: Get on your nerves, don't I? You know what, I bet you never did no double dutching in your day. Strictly a single rope kind of gal.

MARITZA: I played with dolls, mostly.

FATIMA: I figured that's why you wanted to have a baby. It was like your having a real live doll. Marisol is a handful, isn't she?

MARITZA: I don't want to discuss my daughter with you.

FATIMA: Ouch. Odiame. You never told your parents that Derek, sounds like a white boy to me—color me surprised—begged you to marry him. You didn't want to have to share Marisol with him. So you said—

MARITZA: No. Odiame.

FATIMA: Hate me. Si tu me odias quedare yo convencida—I can't push that song out of my mind. I don't know why. Don't you hate when that happens? So, is she a handful or what?

MARITZA: *(After a long pause)* Yes.

FATIMA: De que me amastes mujer con insistencia. She's closer to your mother than she is to you. Pero ten presente, de acuerdo a la experiencia—

MARITZA: She's living with her father now.

FATIMA: You should go out more. Get a life. Have a date every now and then.

MARITZA: You sound just like my mother. She thinks men are the answer to everything.

FATIMA: I never said men. Pero ten presente, de acuerdo a la experiencia. Finish it for me. You know it, don't you?

MARITZA: This is not going to help you or me.

FATIMA: "And bear in mind, as experience has taught us, that you can only hate what you love." So don't feel too bad about sometimes hating your mother and your daughter. And me.

MARITZA: I don't hate you.

FATIMA: Maybe I hate you, too.

MARITZA: I suffer your presence.

FATIMA: Hate is real strong, Maritza. Flip side of love. Strange. It just is. You hate me, don't you, Maritza? *(She offers herself.)* Disappear me. Make me go away. Kiss me as if you could erase me with your lips.

MARITZA: No.

FATIMA: What's that? I'm having a little trouble hearing you.

MARITZA: Is this how you picked the beneficiaries of your healing hand?

(FATIMA *sits facing* MARITZA. *She positions herself to arm wrestle.)*

FATIMA: Winner take all.

MARITZA: Define all.

FATIMA: Milady's hand, s'il vous plait. What do you think, can you take me? Can you take on all those tough girls from the Bronx? Smack-smack-smack.

(MARITZA *sits. They begin to arm wrestle.)*

FATIMA: So tell me, is that your natural hair color or just another feeble stab at assimilation?

MARITZA: Did you like wearing a paper hat to work? How did you get it on your head with your funny hair? Do you have to straighten it much?

FATIMA: Oooh, look at that. The girl can play. Marisol is the daughter you had, ooh how do you almost white people put it, out of wedlock.

MARITZA: You can't read my mind. So how many abortions have you had?

FATIMA: Come in early, stay late. This is it. You've peaked. Still living at home with your parents, waiting for them to die.

(MARITZA *pushes* FATIMA's *hand off center and appears to be winning.*)

FATIMA: Wait, wait, wait. If you can just wait them out you'll be a good daughter. Ooh look at her, she's sweating. Excuse me, perspiring.

MARITZA: Food stamps, welfare, subsidized housing. Sound familiar? Fast food worker was the best you could do, huh? Did they ask for a high-school diploma you didn't have?

(FATIMA *now seems to have the upper hand.*)

FATIMA: You think you're one of them. Newsflash. You are quota. That's all. Quota.

MARITZA: And the Wilfred Beauty Academy was way beyond your intellectual reach.

FATIMA: Unlike you, who rose to the top of the middle.

MARITZA: Where I face people like me—

FATIMA: Like who?

MARITZA: Every single day. I hear them whisper, "She's one of us."

FATIMA: You must have a different script than I do.

MARITZA: And she's going to help us. The old ones will talk to me in Spanish, begging for mercy for their criminal children.

FATIMA: And you feel ashamed.

MARITZA: My father worked two jobs.

FATIMA: The polyester pants, the cheap jewelry. Their idea of dressing up.

MARITZA: I went to Catholic school.

FATIMA: Tried to form a club in your school for Puerto Rican girls.

MARITZA: My father wanted me to mix with the right people.

FATIMA: And all you could come up with was two. Two members don't make up a club.

MARITZA: Down, down, down.

(MARITZA *beats* FATIMA *at arm wrestling. They gasp for air, staring at each other.*)

MARITZA: Did you let me win?

FATIMA: Now would I do that? Do you want to join my gang? Do you want to be a part of me? Aren't you tired of always trying to be better than what you are? Wouldn't you rather just be?

MARITZA: I've got to get out of here.

FATIMA: So go.

MARITZA: Your gang have a name?

FATIMA: The Maritza Cruz Fan Club, Inc.

(MARITZA *laughs.*)

FATIMA: We're looking to franchise. Have a whole chain run by two people. Me and you. Women everywhere trying to be like you instead of the other way around. Hey, doesn't it bite that your mother would rather talk to your dead sister than you? When you sneak into your mother's room, after she's asleep, how often is her face wet? She's crying in her sleep. She's dreaming of release but ain't no one in her house have the guts to set her free. What you're doing to her is punishing her. And if that's what you want, fine. But at least call it what it is.

MARITZA: She's my mother.

FATIMA: Why do you think she calls you Leyda? She's not totally whacked. She knows Leyda's the one who's gone. She's calling her to come get her.

MARITZA: No.

FATIMA: She's calling her to set her free. That's the initiation into the Maritza Cruz Fan Club, Inc: You've got to set somebody free. Your mother. Help your mother, Maritza. Kill her. Tell me you're sure that your mother wants to live. She's waiting for you to off her, Maritza. You're the only one she can count on. If you care for her at all, stop her suffering. The choice is yours—

MARITZA: That's not my choice to make.

FATIMA: —or you can pretend it's not.

MARITZA: I'm not like you. I can't kill people.

FATIMA: Not even your poor, sweet, desperate mother.

MARITZA: I am nothing like you!

FATIMA: Make her pain go away. Leyda would.

(MARITZA *slaps her.*)

MARITZA: I'm so sorry.

FATIMA: Leyda would.

MARITZA: Leyda does not exist.

FATIMA: Ask your mother if she exists. I owe you a slap.

MARITZA: I don't think I'll be able to come here anymore, Fatima. I don't think.... I am not going to share my life with you.

FATIMA: You don't have enough to go around. And I would say it to your face, even as it betrays mine and sheds the tears for both of us. How much do you know me? How much do you know me? I think maybe I don't know you at all. I thought I did. Weren't you the person who was going to pull the splinter from our hearts?

END OF ACT ONE

ACT TWO

(From the darkness, the voices of LUZ, FATIMA, *and* MARITZA *intercut for the following lines.)*

LUZ & FATIMA: ¿Acaso sigue el dolor y si sigue, hasta cuando sigue? ¿Dios mio, hasta cuando? Until when?

MARITZA: Must the pain go on, and if it does, until when? Dear God, until when.

(Lights up on LUZ's *bedroom.* LUZ *and* PITO *are holding each other. He softly sings a lullabye, "Lindo Queruvi [Pretty Cherub]". From the other side of the stage,* MARITZA *enters the living room. She stumbles a bit in an effort to take off her coat and to be as quiet as possible. It is obvious she is a bit drunk.)*

MARITZA: I could just walk up to her and say, "Hey, Mami, you done yet?" I can shoot her and swear she was a prowler. I could suffocate her with one of the pillows she embroidered. Hey Mami, you ready? Hey, Luz, are you waiting for Leyda? *(She reaches into her pocket and retrieves a handful of pretzels she took from the bar.)* I just had one of those, damn it. I wanted the fiesta mix. I don't think it's too much to ask from life to have a little more selection. A little more room for choice. Why do you want to kiss me, Fatima? Why do I want you to kiss me? *(She approaches the outside of* LUZ's *bedroom. She hears* PITO *softly singing.)* No one should love as much as Papi does. She'd trade him in a second for some adventure. If I kill Mami does that mean I'm killing you too, Papi? *(She opens the door just a crack, to watch them.)* Look at him. Will I ever in my life have anybody love me like that? Luz, how can you leave someone who loves you so much? Wherever you go, you think you'll ever find that again? Tell me if you're ready, Mami.

(The interrogation room. JEREMY *and* FATIMA.*)*

FATIMA: What do you mean, she called in sick? She was fine yesterday.

JEREMY: It's probably just one of those twenty-four-hour things. It happens in the real world. Not that you would know.

FATIMA: I don't care if she's dead. Tell her to get her ass in here.

JEREMY: She's not feeling well.

FATIMA: I got that part, Jeremy. What you didn't get was the part where I told you to get her in here.

JEREMY: Fatima, come on. You can talk to me for one lousy day.

FATIMA: No, see, no, no, no, no. You get on the phone, no, better yet, you bring me a phone and I will call her. She's gotta come.

JEREMY: No.

FATIMA: *(Talking to herself)* What's she trying to do to me? She knows I need her.

JEREMY: I said, "No."

*(*FATIMA *turns to face* JEREMY. *It is then that she realizes he has not moved.)*

FATIMA: Get out and get me a goddamn phone!

JEREMY: You can talk to me for one day, or you can go to hell.

(Silence)

FATIMA: August fifteenth.

JEREMY: What?

FATIMA: That's the day you gonna die. You wanna know the year?

(JEREMY *turns to leave.*)

FATIMA: Do you wanna know from what?

JEREMY: (*Softly*) No.

FATIMA: 'Cause I can tell you. I can also tell you how to cheat death. Would you like that, Jeremy? (*She holds out her hand to him.*) You wanna give me your hand so bad. So bad. (*Indicating her hand*) Look, your future, right here in my hand. Your past. Everything about you.

(JEREMY *offers his hand; she takes it.*)

FATIMA: Lissen up, I know everything you're ashamed of. We ain't talking small shit, Jeremy. You got a lot to be ashamed of, don't you?

JEREMY: Let go of my hand.

FATIMA: Things you've been trying to forget your entire life. Does it make you feel naked, Jeremy?

JEREMY: I'll get you the phone.

FATIMA: Is it like when your mother walked in and caught you jerking off or is it worse, 'cause Baby, you've had worse. We both know it. It's almost like I was right there, next to you. Dirty, dirty little Jeremy.

(JEREMY *wrests his hand away.*)

FATIMA: You can't hide anything from me. I know every button to press to make you self destruct. So when I say jump I had better see your ass on the mother-fucking ceiling! Now, Mr Big Shot, you can get me the phone.

*(JEREMY lowers his head and begins to cry, softly.
FATIMA realizes she has gone too far. She tries to touch him.)*

FATIMA: Sssh. It's okay.

JEREMY: Please. Don't touch me. Please. Please. You
keep your hands off my life. You don't know what
I'm about. You don't know what I have to go through.

FATIMA: I do know.

JEREMY: I can scrub myself raw but I'll never be clean.
Have you ever told anybody something nice?

FATIMA: Gimme your hand, little boy.

(He does, as a little boy would.)

FATIMA: What do you want to know?

JEREMY: *(Still childlike)* I don't know.

(She closes her eyes as she raises his hand to her cheek.)

FATIMA: Past or future?

JEREMY: I know my past.

FATIMA: You think you do. All right, the future. You're
in the country, next to this house you're gonna own.
You're barefoot. And you got this beautiful smile on
your face. Happiness isn't this great big thing, you let
yourself feel very happy. It's like this real big weight
has been taken off your shoulders. The race is over.
You won. You're finally good enough.

JEREMY: I feel like my entire life has been one of
"almost", "promising", "competent".

FATIMA: *(Gently)* Almost ain't bad. You are like glass,
Jeremy. I can see right through you. Please, go get me
a phone.

(JEREMY turns to exits. FATIMA grips his hand.)

FATIMA: And lay off the coke. You ain't got the nose for it.

(LUZ's *bedroom.* LUZ *is in her bed. Enter* MARITZA, *wearing an oversized tee shirt and a bathrobe. She is a little hung over. The brightness of* LUZ's *room hurts her eyes.*)

MARITZA: La bendición.

LUZ: Que Dios me la acompañe y bendiga. What are you doing home?

MARITZA: I have a headache. I took a sick day.

LUZ: Hey, I thought I had this sick woman racket covered.

MARITZA: Don't worry, you can have it.

LUZ: I do.

MARITZA: I sent Papi off to visit Tio Moncho. So we're going to spend the day together. I'll give you your bath extra early...and we can rent some videos.

LUZ: No. I want to go outside. You can stay here if you want, but me and Leyda, we got plans.

MARITZA: No, Mami. You and me have plans. Come on, what do you want to do today? We have the whole day to ourselves.

LUZ: No thanks. You go ahead with your father.
Oh, and put on some music on your way out. Leyda!

MARITZA: Mami.

LUZ: Leyda!

MARITZA: Mami, please, I have a headache.

LUZ: See, that's why you can't hang out with Leyda and me. We are going to go and pick ourselves up some men. And men don't like no fragile flowers. Men like to get as good as they give.

MARITZA: Leyda's not here.

LUZ: I'm not stupid! Leyda si es here! You're here, she's here. You go get her.

MARITZA: Do you want me to get lost and just leave Leyda here?

LUZ: Don't get jealous. You're just a different type of woman. You take no chances. Eres mi hijita and I love you, but for a good time I can do better.

MARITZA: Where do you go when you're with Leyda?

LUZ: Most of the time we go dancing. We look like sisters. We wear our colors. Hers is yellow, mine is red with mucho cleavage. We put make-up on each other and pile our hair up. Oh yeah, just so we can make it fall when we dance. Our dresses are glittery and wherever we go we make an entrance. Our walk is famous all over town. We look at everybody as we walk in and everybody, I mean everybody, looks at us. Men buy us drinks and light our cigarettes. Women want to hate us, but they can't 'cause we're so beautiful. The first time we dance, we always do it together. That's after we've turned down everybody, but sweetly, you know, so they'll still ask us later. We dance with each other, Leyda and me, and the room is hypnotized. We dance with every part of us. Little by little people will come and dance next to us; trying to pretend they're dancing with us. And then we turn and face them. We dissolve in their presence. Our turns, our perfume, caresses them. Our sweat pours off us and people fight to wipe our brows. Souvenirs. Proof that they danced with wild animals. I think Leyda bites them sometimes. Not hard, just hard enough to own them. And when everyone is done, when even Leyda can't dance, I'm still dancing. The band is playing just for me and I'm under the perfect white hot light. There is nobody hotter than Luz. I love you, Maritza, but this is not something you can understand. Desire is not in your vocabulary.

MARITZA: Que understand ni understand. I was there, remember?

LUZ: Leyda!

MARITZA: And listen, it's not just the desire she don't get. Our girl Maritza don't know anything about passion.

LUZ: Not like us.

MARITZA: Girlfriend, we wrote the book and hid the pages.

LUZ: So what's on for today? Where are we going to bring men to their knees?

MARITZA: It's like a morgue in here. All this old people music. I'm not old, are you?

(MARITZA *goes to the tape player, she puts on* "Quimbara" *by Celia Cruz.*)

LUZ: ¡Ahora fue!

(MARITZA *begins to dance around the room.*)

MARITZA: Hey, are we hot, Mami? Are we hot?

LUZ: The hottest. I want to dance.

MARITZA: No honey, you save yourself for the paying customers. Don't give anything away for free. Make them beg for it.

LUZ: Can you feel everybody's eyes on us? Look at how much they want us.

(MARITZA *laughs. She is dancing erotically around the room. She corners a floor lamp and pretends she is dancing with someone.*)

LUZ: Go, Leyda, go!

(MARITZA *slowly, seductively takes off her robe. She pulls
her oversized tee shirt from behind, making it appear skin
tight.*)

LUZ: Go, baby.

(*The floor lamp has become a dazzled admirer of* MARITZA *as
Ledya.*)

MARITZA: (*Laughing, as she turns the floor lamp on and off*)
Look, Luz, I'm turning him on.

LUZ: He wants you, he needs you, he has to have you.

(MARITZA *turns her back to the lamp and continues to dance
and flirt with her back to "him".*)

MARITZA: Suffer!

LUZ: Go, baby. And take me with you. Get me my
make-up and jewelry.

(MARITZA *goes to her mother's vanity table. There she gets
a tray of make-up and the jewelry box that she brings over to*
LUZ.)

LUZ: (*Referring to the floor lamp*) I think he wants to buy
us a drink.

MARITZA: When we're good and ready.

LUZ: We're always good and we're always ready.

(*Everything about* MARITZA *is heightened sexuality—the
way she moves, sits. She is cruising an imaginary dance club,
filled with people.*)

LUZ: Nena, the mirror.

MARITZA: No, Luz. You don't need no mirror.
I'll be your mirror.

(MARITZA *begins to apply make-up to* LUZ.)

LUZ: I want a beauty mark by my mouth.

MARITZA: Nena, I know. I ain't no amateur.

(The phone rings. It rattles MARITZA, *who is momentarily frozen in place.)*

LUZ: Tell them we're not ready yet.

MARITZA: What?

LUZ: Leyda, just tell them to wait.

*(*MARITZA *goes to turn off the music.)*

LUZ: Ni te atrevas. You know I don't get gorgeous without my music. Have them send over a drink while you're up.

*(*MARITZA *answers the phone, covering the mouthpiece.)*

MARITZA: Yeah, well, the day we have to start buying drinks for ourselves is the day.... *(She fades.)*

LUZ: *(Laughing, oblivious)* Sangana.

MARITZA: *(As herself, into phone)* Hello.

FATIMA: What the hell is going on there? You got yourself a party going?

*(*MARITZA *hangs up.)*

MARITZA: I gotta lower it. Just a little.

LUZ: Okay, but just a little.

*(*MARITZA *does. The phone rings again. She answers it.)*

FATIMA: *(Softly)* Hey Maritza. *(No answer)* You playing Leyda for Mami? *(No answer)* That's a good girl.

LUZ: *(While applying lipstick)* Tell them I'll need fifteen more minutes.

FATIMA: Tell her she's got it, but not a minute more.

MARITZA: Si, Luz, okay.

FATIMA: Where's she off to?

MARITZA: We're going dancing.

Luz: Ahora fue.

Fatima: And when the pain becomes unbearable she'll cry herself to sleep, but for now, she's going dancing.

Maritza: Yeah.

Fatima: So.

Maritza: So.

Fatima: My splinter says hello. What's your splinter doing?

Maritza: She's putting on jewelry. Lots of it.

(Luz *tries to clasp a necklace behind her neck. Her hands begin to tremble. She tries, but cannot stop the trembling. She knocks everything off her bed and begins to weep.* Maritza *drops the phone and takes* Luz *in her arms.*)

Luz: ¿Hasta cuándo? ¿Dios mio, hasta cuándo?

(Maritza *coos to her mother.*)

Maritza: Sssh, Luz. It's okay, Mami.

Luz: No, it's not okay. I have never been out of this room. I will never be allowed out. My whole childhood, Puerto Rico, my freedom is all a fantasy. What is God waiting for?

(Maritza *and* Luz *hug tightly in the bed. The music ends.*)

Luz: I never wanted to be a burden. A shadow of what I was.

Maritza: What do you want me to do, Mami? Just tell me. I'll do anything you say.

Luz: Don't go without me, Leyda.

(Maritza, *as if slapped, slowly backs away from* Luz. *She gets up from the bed and in her bare feet she steps on one of* Luz's *earrings. With a fury not pertaining to this, she hurls it against the wall, where it shatters.*)

MARITZA: ¡Puñeta!

(LUZ *continues sobbing.* MARITZA *picks up the phone receiver from the floor. She is about to replace it in its cradle, but almost against her will brings it to her ear.*)

FATIMA: Haven't you ever wanted to go dancing, Maritza? That's all she wants, to have some control over her body. It's what you want, it's what I want. Let her dance.

MARITZA: That's not my choice to make.

FATIMA: Then you dance with me.

MARITZA: No. I have to go now.

FATIMA: Please. Please come back.

LUZ: Leyda, don't go without me.

FATIMA: I want to give you, Maritza, my love.
Me, Fatima, I want to love you, Maritza. Maritza.

(MARITZA *hangs up. Lights down on* FATIMA.
MARITZA *begins to pick up her mother's jewelry. Fade.*)

(*The interrogation room.* FATIMA *is there. Enter* PAUL.)

FATIMA: You short a headline?

PAUL: Every headline on the button. (*He stares at her a moment, then takes a flask from his jacket pocket. He takes a drink.*)

FATIMA: You big man on campus now?

PAUL: Yeah.

FATIMA: Feel good?

PAUL: Very good.

(PAUL *offers her a drink. She refuses.*)

PAUL: Go ahead. Live a little.

FATIMA: Paul, are you trying to get me drunk?

PAUL: *(Small laugh)* No.

FATIMA: Are you drunk?

PAUL: I don't get drunk.

FATIMA: You probably gonna tell me you don't go to the bathroom, neither.

PAUL: Haven't you heard? I'm Superman.

FATIMA: A word to the wise, a big ego and a small dick is a dangerous combination. Don't be blinded by your own light.

PAUL: Save that for you.

FATIMA: Excuse me? *(Silence)* Hey, Paulie, why are you here? Come to kiss me goodbye or you maybe wanna ask me something? Is that why you're drinking, to get the old courage up? You wanna ask the spic something?

(PAUL *thrusts his hand out.*)

PAUL: I dare you to find that word in me! I come here, I work here. I try to help the people here. What am I doing wrong? Spell it out for me. I don't belong? I have no right to be here?

FATIMA: Ding ding ding ding ding. We have a winner.

PAUL: When did I become the enemy? Can't bring my car to work without fear of—

FATIMA: Man, at least you got—

PAUL: —without fear of it being stripped in broad daylight. Attitude from Blacks and Hispanics, no, Latinos, uh, Spanish. How the hell am I supposed to refer to you this week?

(FATIMA *offers her hand;* PAUL *takes it.*)

FATIMA: You get *one* question.

PAUL: Don't tell me about the graffiti at my expense. I already know that. Don't tell me about the cashier at the bodega who won't acknowledge me even though I learned how to say "gracias" just for her.

FATIMA: I'll try to skip it.

PAUL: All I want is a yes or no answer, that's all. What I want to know is...

FATIMA: If you can't look at me turn away.

(PAUL *does.*)

FATIMA: Surprise me.

PAUL: Will the loneliness ever end?

(FATIMA *is stunned out of her flippancy.*)

PAUL: The last time I was in love I was, what? Twenty-five. You can laugh if you want to, it's okay.

FATIMA: I'm not laughing.

PAUL: When you get older you can actually pinpoint who was the love of your life. The one. The real thing. How was I supposed to know? I was twenty-five, for Christ's sake. *(Silence)* So, I guess my question is.... Forget it, I don't want to know. Sometimes I feel like I've been betrayed by my own life.

FATIMA: Wow, Paul. We finally match.

(*The interrogation room.* FATIMA *is seated. Enter* MARITZA. FATIMA *rises.*)

FATIMA: Hi. *(Silence)* I thought maybe I had scared you off. Wondered if I would ever see you again. *(Silence)* I mean, just because I can't get her out of my mind doesn't mean she hasn't forgotten me already. What do you think? *(Silence)* What can I give her? You. What can I give you? Some memories you may not even want to have? *(Silence)* You got me biting my nails here. All because of you. Hey, are you gonna say something or

are you just gonna try to stare me down? 'Cause, honey,
if that's the case you're way out of your league.

(Silence. FATIMA *reaches out for* MARITZA's *hands.*
MARITZA *pulls back.* FATIMA *sits on the floor and begins to
play patty cake with herself, slapping her hands together and
against her thighs.)*

FATIMA: You are the best best best of all the rest rest rest
and you will be be be the one for me me me. Second
verse, same as the first. You are the best best best of all
the rest rest rest and you will be be be the one for me
me me. Jump in anytime. Ma-rit-za Ma-rit-za, this is
kind of lonely, Ma-rit-za. Only one way to find out,
Ma-rit-za. I dare you.

*(*MARITZA *smiles.)*

FATIMA: I double dare you, Ma-rit-za.

*(*MARITZA *kneels in front of* FATIMA *and slowly joins in.*
FATIMA *tries to slow down to allow* MARITZA *to catch up
to her.* MARITZA *misses a couple of times.)*

FATIMA: Shit, and I had such a good head of steam
going.

(Then, the unexpected happens, MARITZA *picks up speed,
leaving* FATIMA *in the dust.)*

FATIMA: Whoa girl, you gonna get wind burns.

*(*MARITZA's *speed increases.)*

MARITZA: Fa-ti-ma, keep up with me. Fa-ti-ma, don't be
afraid. I won't hurt you, Fa-ti-ma.

FATIMA: Hold up.

*(*MARITZA *complicates her routine.)*

MARITZA: Close your eyes.

FATIMA: Honey, just 'cause I may sometimes look
stupid, don't mean—

MARITZA: Close your eyes and follow me, Fa-ti-ma.

(FATIMA *does. It is then that she is able to finally match* MARITZA.)

MARITZA: I won't let you fall, Fa-ti-ma. I won't let you fall, Fa-ti-ma. I won't let you—

(FATIMA *opens her eyes and pulls her hands back.*)

FATIMA: It's out of your hands.

(MARITZA *begins to slap herself.* FATIMA *tries to hold down her hands.*)

FATIMA: Hey, come on, don't do that.

MARITZA: It's okay. I'm not a good person, you know. I'm not. I'm not!

(MARITZA *hits herself again.* FATIMA *grabs her hand.*)

MARITZA: Hey, Fatima, who would I be taking out of their misery, me or my mother? And where do I hide my smile of relief?

FATIMA: On your mother's lips. Or on mine.

(FATIMA *kisses* MARITZA's *palm, closes it and puts it against* MARITZA's *heart.* MARITZA *takes* FATIMA's *head in her hands. She kisses her forehead.*)

FATIMA: I'm scared.

MARITZA: Me too. I'm not going to be able to go back to nothing again.

(MARITZA *kisses* FATIMA *on the mouth.* FATIMA *shudders and braces herself to feel pain.*)

FATIMA: ...painless...

MARITZA: Give me your hands.

FATIMA: There was no Coco. No nobodys. You'll be the first and the last.

MARITZA: No past. No future.

(MARITZA takes FATIMA's hands and runs them on her body. FATIMA exhales in pleasure.)

MARITZA: Welcome home.

(Fade. Lights slowly up on LUZ's bedroom. LUZ is in her bed. Enter PITO. He very quietly approaches LUZ and is about to kiss her.)

LUZ: I'm awake.

PITO: *(Startled)* Jesus Cristo.

LUZ: What? You thought I died in my sleep?

PITO: Of course not. Did you take your medicine yet?

LUZ: No, old man, I haven't.

(PITO pours her a glass of water.)

PITO: Why don't you take your pill and try to go to sleep. You don't want to be awake when the pain hits you. I guarantee it.

LUZ: Look who he's telling. You want to spend the night here tonight?

PITO: I don't want to keep you up. I snore, I move around a lot.

LUZ: Maybe I want to be kept up. Come on, you're not that old, old man. Are all your working parts still working?

(LUZ playfully grabs for PITO, who backs away.)

LUZ: I'm not too attractive to you right now, am I?

PITO: Come on, Lucesita, take your medicine for daddy.

LUZ: My daddy's in Puerto Rico. Where's yours? How about a kiss? *(PITO does not respond.)* Come on, just one. A quick peck, mi amor.

(PITO leans in for a quick kiss; LUZ grabs at him.)

PITO: Okay, okay, that's enough.

LUZ: I smell like death, huh? That's okay. You smell old. Together we smell like what my grandparents used to smell like.

PITO: Come on, take your medicine.

LUZ: I want to go to the window. Please, Pito.

PITO: Estás que no hay quien te beba el caldo esta noche.

LUZ: Yeah, well, you too. Window, please.

PITO: I'm not, I'm not, I'm not. No.

LUZ: I'll take the medicine with me.

PITO: Spoiled. Just like a little girl.

LUZ: Well take a look in the mirror at the one who spoiled me.

(PITO *picks up* LUZ, *who dutifully takes her medicine with her. He carries her to the window.)*

PITO: Okay, now take (your medicine.)

LUZ: Put me down on the window sill. What's the matter with you?

PITO: Cuidado.

LUZ: Open the window. I want to see the stars.

PITO: You can see the stars just fine the way it is.

(LUZ *tries to open the window.* PITO *stops her.)*

LUZ: With my hands or with my head I am going to open that window.

(PITO *opens the window. He puts his arms around her waist to hold her in place. She inhales deeply.)*

PITO: Is my Lucesita happy now?

(LUZ *makes as if she is going to spit out the window.)*

PITO: Don't you dare.

LUZ: It's six flights. We have enough time to get back inside and they won't even see who did it. I bet you marry another teenager when I'm gone.

PITO: I'm not a young man anymore.

LUZ: You never were. Let me know when you get tired of holding me.

PITO: Never.

LUZ: You see that star? I bet I could reach it. It's not as far away as it looks. *(She stretches her arm.)* I almost got it. I can feel it brush against my fingertips.

(PITO kisses the back of her head.)

PITO: I won't let you fall.

LUZ: I know you won't.

PITO: *(Singing softly)* Duerme muñequita—

LUZ: I have always hated that song. *(She jerks, involuntarily, in pain.)*

PITO: Come on, it's time for your medicine.

(LUZ opens the bottle of pills and pours them out the window. PITO tries to stop her, then tries to retrieve some of the pills.)

PITO: Luz!

(He momentarily loosens his grip on her. LUZ spreads her arms as if she were going to fly away. She laughs.)

PITO: Luz!

(LUZ flaps her "wings".)

LUZ: How do butterflies do this?

PITO: Come on, get inside, now. Right now.

LUZ: It's okay, Pito. I can do this. I've seen butterflies do this.

(PITO *carries her to her bed and tries to calm himself.*)

PITO: God is the only one who can say when it's time for you to leave me. You do not get a vote. You are not allowed to do this! (*He falls to his knees and begins to pray.*) Ave Maria Purísima, pecado inconcebido, Santa Maria, madre de Dios, ruega señora por nosotros los pecadores—

(LUZ, *with great difficulty, caresses his head.*)

LUZ: I know you mean well, old man.

PITO: ...ahora en la hora de nuestra muerte, amen.

(*The interrogation room.* FATIMA *and* MARITZA *sit holding hands.*)

FATIMA: I would take my crazy drunk uncle's hand and spook him. He was afraid of me. Afraid of this skinny six-year-old girl. He'd be carrying on, destroying everything, making everybody cry and his wife would come and get me. I'd walk up to him and hold out my hand and he'd get in a corner and start to scream and I would start telling all this stuff about him. It was neat. I was his bogey man. Then he jumped off our building. He took me to the roof and grabbed my hand and tried to pull me with him but I got loose. Everybody in my family knew it was because of me but no one said anything. At his funeral I'm staring at the crucifix with the nails that go through our Father's hands and I wonder if he's trying to tell me something. I'm six years old, I don't know. I never owned this, this has always owned me.

(PAUL *and* JEREMY *enter.* PAUL *hands a thick manila folder to* MARITZA *from which she will pull out papers for* FATIMA *to sign throughout the course of the scene.*)

PAUL: This just states that you were made fully aware of your rights, and...

(He waits for MARITZA *to hand* FATIMA *a document to sign. She does not.)*

PAUL: Maritza, please.

*(*MARITZA *puts the paper in front of* FATIMA.*)*

PAUL: —that you chose to waive them. You were in no way coerced and no promises were made to you.

JEREMY: There are a couple of people interested in buying the rights to your story. You of course know that in New York the criminal cannot profit from his...or her crime. The estates of the victims would share equally in any profits your story might bring.

PAUL: And sign here.

*(*MARITZA *places another paper in front of* FATIMA. *She signs it.)*

PAUL: There'll be some psychiatric tests done on you. Procedure. Just to prove you're not nuts, that's all.

JEREMY: There are a couple of entrances to the courthouse that we can take to try to avoid a free-for-all, but any way you look at it we're talking freak show.

PAUL: We will do the best we can, but they've been waiting for you.

(The lights fade, encircling FATIMA *and* MARITZA. *There is a long pause, where* MARITZA *tries to smooth* FATIMA's *brow.* FATIMA *gently shakes her off.)*

FATIMA: I'm gonna be locked away forever in some place with people pawing at me. Begging me to read their lives. Everybody's hand stretched out to me. What will I do when it hurts just to touch myself?

*(*MARITZA *places another document to be signed in front of her. As before,* FATIMA *signs it without looking at it. She places her hands in her lap.)*

FATIMA: When clothing weighs heavy on my skin and I can feel the anguish of my hair and nails growing. When the air burns me when I breathe. They'll put me in a straight jacket. And all I'll hear from morning to night will be one long scream. Mine. I can see my future. Maritza, you have to help me.

(MARITZA *slowly puts her hand under the table. She takes* FATIMA'*s hand.*)

(*From the darkness* FATIMA *appears behind* LUZ. MARITZA *enters, carrying a tray with a plate of food. She sees* FATIMA. *For a moment they stare at each other, then very gently* FATIMA *begins to brush* LUZ'*s hair. When* MARITZA *goes toward her,* FATIMA *disappears.*)

LUZ: ¿Y tu padre?

MARITZA: He's resting.

LUZ: He gets tired so easy now. He always had so much energy. Call him in here.

MARITZA: Okay. Papi.

(PITO *enters.*)

LUZ: I'm still waiting for my magazines, old man.

PITO: It's raining, Luz. I'm waiting until it stops raining.

LUZ: Lucky you. You can wait.

MARITZA: I'll get them.

LUZ: This is between your father and me. A few magazines for a life. He's getting off cheap. Go on, tell Maritza how you stole my life, old man.

PITO: Vamos Lucesita.

LUZ: No, Lucesita here, old man. This is a woman in this bed. But you don't like women—

MARITZA: Come on, Mami—

LUZ: —no, you like little girls. Little girls who don't know what a real man feels like. Nothing to compare you to.

MARITZA: Papi, go outside.

PITO: I love you, Lucesita.

LUZ: I wish you were dead! I wish it was you in this bed. Tubes running in and out of your body and all I'd have to do is squeeze one of them to put me out of my misery.

(PITO kisses LUZ and goes to door.)

LUZ: Pito...don't forget my magazines.

PITO: Te amo. *(He exits.)*

LUZ: Me too.

(MARITZA is trying to contain her anger. She puts the dinner tray down. She is unable to face LUZ.)

LUZ: Pain absolves my sins.

(MARITZA whips the sheet off LUZ.)

LUZ: I'm cold!

MARITZA: Too bad.

LUZ: I'm cold.

MARITZA: He's gone out in the rain now to get you some stinking magazines. He'll go from store to store until he finds some you haven't pawed over and bring them back as if he's discovered some buried treasure for his little princess.

LUZ: And he'll be tired. He'll go to bed and be good as new tomorrow. I would trade places with him anytime.

(MARITZA gives her the dinner tray.)

LUZ: Aren't you going to eat?

MARITZA: I'm not hungry.... Maybe you'll let me have some of yours, Mami.

LUZ: You would eat from my plate?

MARITZA: Of course.

LUZ: I'm still cold.

(MARITZA *covers her with the sheet.*)

LUZ: Lay in bed with me.

(MARITZA *climbs into bed with* LUZ.)

LUZ: You're real quiet.

MARITZA: I'm sorry.

LUZ: Y Marisol?

MARITZA: I called her. She had some of her little friends over so we couldn't talk much. She's happy to be living with her father.

LUZ: She should be with you. A daughter needs her mother.

MARITZA: Yeah, I guess sometimes.

LUZ: (*She tastes her food.*) It's good.

MARITZA: Is it? My mind kept wandering while I was cooking.

LUZ: No, it's very very good. Very good. Taste it.

MARITZA: Later.

LUZ: Okay, later. 'Cause it's good, you know.

MARITZA: Uh-huh.

(LUZ *puts her plate aside*)

MARITZA: Eat it, don't just let it get cold, Mami.

LUZ: I'll wait for you so we can eat together.

(MARITZA *takes a hurried mouthful.*)

MARITZA: I ate, okay? Now finish it. If you don't want to eat just leave it there and let it rot.

(LUZ *begins to cry.*)

MARITZA: I'm sorry.

LUZ: I know I've been a bad mother.

MARITZA: No, you haven't.

LUZ: I tried, Maritza.

MARITZA: Look, I'll eat some, okay? See? I'm eating. Now you eat, too. You want me to get Leyda?

LUZ: *(Laughs)* Leyda's dead! Car crash, she's scattered all over Grand Concourse. Social clubs in the Bronx are going to have a moment of silence in her honor.

MARITZA: Mami, please.

LUZ: How do you kill somebody who's already dead, huh, Maritza? It's not easy. I can't do it, can you? Pobrecita. Pieces of Leyda everywhere. And who do you think was driving the car, Maritza? Who do you think?!

(LUZ *convulses in pain.* MARITZA *gets her medicine.*)

MARITZA: Hold on, Mami. Hold on.

LUZ: She's in my headlights. She sees me coming and all she does is smile. And she's flying. Last night I tried to fly. Like a butterfly.

MARITZA: You didn't kill anybody.

LUZ: There are no butterflies in the Bronx.

MARITZA: Come on, take your medicine.

(LUZ *takes the pill from her and holds it in her hand. She takes the capsule and opens it and pours it on her food.*)

LUZ: I kept hoping there was something else for me to do, but there isn't. Last night, the stars told me. I'm

done. Over. You call my sisters, oistes? You shouldn't
have to take care of your father alone. He's a handful.

(MARITZA *lowers her head and begins to cry.* LUZ *stretches,*
trying to reach the bottle of pills.)

LUZ: Maritza, you're going to have to help me here.
I can't reach it.

MARITZA: Mami.

LUZ: In my sleep, Maritza, I feel so light. Last night
was the first night I spent without medicine. Terrible.
I couldn't sleep. I would stuff the pillow in my mouth
so I could scream.

(MARITZA *gives her the bottle.* LUZ *takes a pill and empties*
it onto her food.)

LUZ: I feel so light. And I kept thinking what I wouldn't
give to die in my sleep. 'Cause, that's so peaceful. You
just forget to wake up. Pieces of Leyda everywhere.
Wearing her butterfly costume. I could never do that.
Never. Help me. Just one pill for Mami.

(MARITZA *opens a pill and empties it into the food.*)

MARITZA: Mami, what if I want you to go?

LUZ: Then help me.

(LUZ *leans back, exhausted.* MARITZA *continues to empty*
the pills onto the food.)

MARITZA: (*Singing softly*) Duerme muñequita guarda
bien de tu querer—Mami, sing with me. (LUZ *is silent.*)
I used to love singing. I thought I had a beautiful voice,
just like yours. And I so much wanted to be like you.
My movie star mother who sang by the window. But
you started getting headaches. So it became, "Can you
sing softer, Maritza." Softer. Softer.

LUZ: I feel so light.

MARITZA: Singing as soft as I could, but it was still too loud. Even if all I did was mouth the words you swore you could hear me. So I would wait until you were singing your songs in Spanish and I would hide in the corner of your closet...and sing. Very softly. Love songs to your party dresses. I never stopped wishing you would open the door and say, "What a beautiful voice. Come sing with me. *(She has emptied the last pill onto the food.)* Is this for you or for me? *(She gets up with the plate and heads for the door)*

LUZ: Maritza, please, come sing with me.

(MARITZA sits by LUZ. LUZ tries to feed herself, but she is too weak and spills a spoonful.)

LUZ: Your father will move my bed to the window so I can see the stars. I hunger for them, Maritza.

(MARITZA gives LUZ a spoonful of food.)

LUZ: I feel so light.

(MARITZA feeds LUZ.)

LUZ: You sing, but I'll dance.

MARITZA: Okay, Mami, I'll sing.

(Fade to PITO in black, praying, on his knees.)

PITO: Ave Maria Purísima, pecado inconcebido. Dios te salve Maria, llena eres de gracia, el Señor es contigo, bendita tu eres, entre todas las mujeres, aqui y en el cielo bendito sea el fruto de tu vientre, Jesus....

(PITO fades, FATIMA replaces him.)

FATIMA: Holy Mary, mother of God, pray for us sinners, now, in the hour of our death, amen.

(FATIMA continues praying, silently. She will occasionally convulse with pain. JEREMY and PAUL appear on either side of the stage. They do not see her. MARITZA enters, carrying the plate, and stands a few feet behind FATIMA. PAUL and

JEREMY *speak to* MARITZA; *their voices rise and fall.*
They are oblivious of everyone but MARITZA.)

JEREMY: The department, your co-workers, and I
myself would like to offer our most sincere condolences
regarding the unfortunate demise of your mother. In
this time of loss it's always best to remember the good
things.

PAUL: Maritza, rumors get around. People talk.
Nothing is secret. Don't think people don't know about
you and Fatima. I've heard things. Things I wouldn't
acknowledge because I thought too highly of you.

JEREMY: She died in her sleep, that's how I want to go.

PAUL: The stress of having to care for your mother may
have led to some temporary lapses in judgment on your
part.

MARITZA: I feel so light.

JEREMY: She's at peace now. That's what you have to
think. If there's anything, anything I can do.

PAUL: Your relationship with Ms Garcia is something
that will not leave this room. I also must inform you
that your participation in this case is as of now officially
over.

MARITZA: If his lips are moving why can't I hear him
sing?

PAUL: Cause of death, probable suicide.

(JEREMY *and* PAUL *disappear.* MARITZA *takes a few steps
toward* FATIMA. MARITZA *touches* FATIMA; *her pain ends.*)

MARITZA: I've come for my splinter, Fatima. When does
your need to leave surpass my need to touch? When do
I love enough to let go? *(Pause)* Will it be easier than the
first one?

FATIMA: Painless.

(MARITZA *kneels and begins to feed* FATIMA, *who places her hand on* MARITZA's *heart.*)

MARITZA: Painless. I promise you. And my heart will break. But I will get over you, my darling, I really will. Someday.

END OF PLAY

CPSIA information can be obtained
at www.ICGtesting.com
Printed in the USA
LVHW080405101219
639927LV00014BA/1371/P